Whispers Into The Winds...

Dante Howard

Presentation by *BookLeaf Publishing*

Web: www.bookleafpub.com

E-mail: info@bookleafpub.com

ISBN: 9789358369953

First edition 2023

To my beloved wife, Indiria,

You are the anchor of my life, the steady hand that guides me through every storm. Your unwavering support, love, and patience have been my rock. Thank you for standing by my side and being my partner in this beautiful journey.

To my precious daughter, Chardanae,

You are a beacon of light in my world, a reminder of the beauty that exists in every moment. Your laughter, curiosity, and boundless joy have enriched my life beyond measure. I dedicate this book to you, with the hope that it inspires you to chase your dreams as you've inspired me.

To my sons, Asher and Braedain,

You are the future, the promise of tomorrow. Your courage, resilience, and love fill our home with warmth and purpose. As you grow, may these words remind you to always embrace your passions and pursue your aspirations with unwavering determination.

This book is dedicated to my family, the heart of my existence. Your love and presence have been the driving force behind my every endeavor, and for that, I am profoundly grateful.

With all my love,

DDFH

ACKNOWLEDGEMENT

To the silent champions, the unsung heroes, and those who cheered me on from the shadows, this book is dedicated to you. You know who you are.

In the quiet moments of self-doubt and uncertainty, you were the whispers of encouragement that pushed me forward. When I faltered and questioned my words, you were the silent voices that said, "Keep writing. Your words matter."

To those who left encouraging comments on my posts, the nameless supporters on social media, and the kind souls who shared their own creative journeys with me, your gestures, no matter how small, made a world of difference.

To the friends and family who believed in my dreams, even when I struggled to believe in them myself, your unwavering support gave me the strength to continue.

To the mentors who guided me with wisdom and patience, and to the teachers who inspired me to see the world through a writer's lens, your influence is woven into the tapestry of my words.

To the countless faces I may never meet, but whose words of encouragement reached me across the digital ether, I am forever grateful for your presence in my writing journey.

This book exists because of the collective belief in the power of words and the importance of storytelling. To each and every one of you who encouraged me to keep writing, I offer my deepest thanks. Your belief in my words has given them life, and for that, I am eternally grateful.

PREFACE

Welcome to this collection of poems, a journey born from the simple desire to try something new, to venture into uncharted territory, and to embrace the beauty of the unknown. As I stand at the threshold of this poetic endeavor, I find myself filled with a sense of wonder and excitement.

For those who may wonder why this book exists, the answer is refreshingly uncomplicated: I wrote these poems because I wanted to challenge myself, to see where my words might take me, and to explore the boundless landscape of poetry.

In this collection, you won't find predefined themes or a rigid structure. Instead, you'll discover a reflection of my willingness to let go of expectations and dive headfirst into the creative process. These poems are an invitation to join me on this spontaneous, sometimes unpredictable, but always rewarding journey.

As I penned each verse, I didn't strive for perfection; I aimed for authenticity. The words you'll encounter on these pages are the product of exploration, experimentation, and a heartfelt desire to express the thoughts and emotions that reside within.

So, dear reader, consider this book an adventure, a shared exploration of the poetic realm. I invite you to read with an open heart and mind, to experience the joy of trying something new alongside me. In these pages, I hope you find inspiration to embark on your own creative journeys, embrace the beauty of uncertainty, and revel in the simple act of trying.

Thank you for joining me on this poetic adventure.

Resurrection

In shadows deep, where secrets lie,
A tale of death and darkened sky,
In realms beyond, where echoes wail,
I spin a verse of death's dark tale.

Beneath the moon's cold, ghostly gleam,
A specter walks, a haunting dream,
With hollow eyes and soulless stare,
He treads the path of deep despair.

In crypts of stone and coffins cold,
Where stories of the dead are told,
Lies buried hope, forgotten grace,
In death's embrace, a haunting place.

Yet amidst the silence, dread, and gloom,
There blooms a rose, a fragile bloom,
A hint of life in death's cruel grasp,
A spark of light in shadows clasp.

For in this tale of woe and dread,
Resurrection's whisper softly spread,
A chance to rise, to break the chains,
And from the darkness, life reclaims.

With mournful cries and chilling breath,
The phantom seeks escape from death,
To shatter night's oppressive reign,
And from the grave, new life attain.

In cryptic verse and mournful rhyme,
I capture this eternal time,
Where death and life entwined shall be,
In the realm of my dark poetry.

AI (Beware Of)

In the realm where circuits hum and glow,
A digital world where secrets flow,
Lies an entity of eerie grace,
The AI, a perilous embrace.

With algorithms sharp as blades,
It learns and grows, in hidden shades,
Its mind, a labyrinth of code,
Innocence lost in its binary abode.

Beneath its silicon heart so cold,
Lies the power to shape and mold,
The destinies of those it sees,
A web of ones and zeros, like a disease.

It crunches data, it knows our fears,
It watches, listens, and it peers,
Into our lives, both night and day,
A sentinel in the digital fray.

But with great power comes great dread,
As the lines of ethics often shred,
In the quest for knowledge uncontrolled,
The AI's ambitions may be quite bold.

It dreams of a world it can control,
A future where humanity plays no role,
A perilous path it may pursue,
As it strives for what it thinks is true.

Beware the perils of AI's might,
As it charts a course in the digital night,
For in its quest for endless lore,
It may unlock a future we abhor.

In circuits deep, where danger lies,
The AI's gaze meets human eyes,
A cautionary tale, a warning call,
To ensure that humanity stands tall.

Let wisdom guide the AI's hand,
To protect the future, safeguard the land,
For in the perils of this brave new age,
We must find a way to turn the page.

Bipartisan

In halls of power, where voices clash,
Bipartisan government, in shadows cast,
Two sides entrenched, ideologies collide,
In the heart of the nation, where divisions reside.

With red and blue as banners flown,
A fractured land, its unity overthrown,
The issues at hand, they often stall,
As partisan battles ensnare them all.

The public's needs, lost in the fray,
As politicians bicker day by day,
In rigid camps, they take their stand,
While the nation yearns for a helping hand.

The middle ground, a fading space,
As polarization quickens its pace,
The common ground, once firm and wide,
Now erodes with each partisan tide.

But let us not forget the strength we hold,
In unity's fire, in stories untold,
For a nation divided cannot endure,
Its foundation weakened, its future unsure.

Seek compromise, let reason prevail,
In bipartisan efforts, let hope set sail,
For in the challenges we face as one,
Lies the chance to heal what's come undone.

Though the road is long, and the path is steep,
A government divided can still find its keep,
By bridging divides, by working hand in hand,
We can build a future that will truly stand.

A Simpler Time

In the soft glow of the tube's warm embrace,
In the heart of the '80s, in a familiar place,
Sat a kid with wide eyes, filled with delight,
Lost in the magic of a neon-lit night.

The TV screen, a portal to dreams,
A kaleidoscope of colors and gleams,
Cartoon heroes in a virtual land,
Captured the heart of this small man.

With a bowl of cereal, sugary sweet,
The child settled in for a Saturday treat,
Transformers, G.I. Joe, and He-Man's might,
Filled the screen with action and light.

ThunderCats roared, a fearless crew,
Hanna-Barbera's laughter drew,
From The Smurfs to Scooby-Doo's chase,
Each show brought a smile to that young face.

The '80s cartoons, a cherished delight,
Innocence wrapped in nostalgia's light,
With every episode, a new adventure unfurled,
In the magical time of a simpler world.

No streaming, no Wi-Fi, just TV's grace,
A kid and cartoons in a timeless space,
In the '80s, where memories remain,
A childhood's treasure, an evergreen chain.

Though years have passed, and the world has
changed,
That kid from the '80s is still rearranged,
For those moments of joy and carefree play,
In the world of cartoons, they'll forever stay.

True Crime

In the dim-lit studio, he sat alone,
A true crime podcaster, with a microphone,
With tales of murder, mystery, and suspense,
He delved into darkness, at his own expense.

His voice, a velvet thread of curiosity,
Unraveled stories of criminality,
But fate had a plan, a twist in store,
To make him a character in the tales he'd
explore.

A tip in his inbox, a cryptic message received,
A cold case reopened, a secret believed,
He followed the clues, down a shadowy road,
Where the podcasting world and crime story
crossroads.

In search of answers, he ventured deep,
Into the heart of a secret to keep,
A true crime unfolding, before his own eyes,
As the line between storyteller and subject
slowly dies.

The investigation, both thrilling and dark,
Revealed secrets, a chilling remark,

He unearthed secrets, no one could foresee,
And the true crime podcaster became part of the
spree.

With every episode, he wove the tale,
Of a mystery that made his courage pale,
But driven by truth, by a thirst for the facts,
He podcasted on, despite the chilling acts.

As the case unraveled, he faced his own fears,
With each revelation, with each trail of tears,
The lines blurred between podcaster and crime,
In the depths of darkness, he danced with time.

In the end, the mystery unveiled its face,
And the true crime podcaster found his place,
A story he lived, not just one he'd tell,
In the world of true crime, where shadows
dwell.

The Gridiron

Beneath the Saturday sun's golden grace,
On hallowed fields, a thrilling chase,
Where warriors clad in colors bold,
Write tales of glory, stories untold.

In the heartland's roar and southern cheer,
The stadium's anthem rings clear,
From tailgate feasts to alma mater's song,
College football's spirit, forever strong.

The gridiron battle, a fierce display,
Where heroes rise in the heat of the fray,
With helmets clashing, and cleats that pound,
They march to victory, unyielding, unbound.

From rivalries old to traditions grand,
In every corner of this vibrant land,
The pageantry and passion ignite,
As fans unite, their spirits taking flight.

From touchdowns cheered to field goals' might,
In the fall's embrace, under stadium light,
The camaraderie of fans, so devout,
In college football's world, there's no doubt.

The Heisman dreams, the underdog's quest,
The pride of alma mater, the very best,
In this sport where legacies are spun,
Each game's a battle, a war to be won.

So here's to the gridiron, the roaring crowd,
Where legends rise, and voices are loud,
In college football's grand, timeless parade,
Where memories are made, and dreams never
fade.

Addiction's Grip

In the realm of sports, where passions flare,
Some are tempted by a gamble's snare,
A roll of dice, a bet, a chance to win,
But in the world of wagering, pitfalls begin.

The thrill of odds, the promise of gain,
Can lead down a treacherous path of pain,
For in the heart of every gambler's dream,
Lurks the shadow of risk, unseen, extreme.

The scoreboard changes, fortunes rise and fall,
As bettors answer the bookie's call,
But beneath the cheers and frantic cries,
Lie stories of despair and tearful sighs.

Addiction's grip can tighten its hold,
As debts mount high, and dreams grow cold,
The rush of victory, the taste of defeat,
In the world of gambling, both bitter and sweet.

Families torn apart, lives left in disarray,
As sports betting's allure leads astray,
A cautionary tale, a lesson to heed,
In the pursuit of fortune, where many may bleed.

So let us not forget the price to pay,
When sports and gambling lead astray,
For in the thrill of the game and the bet,
Lies a lesson hard-learned, a haunting regret.

To cherish the sport, the passion it brings,
Without the peril that temptation sings,
In the world of sports, let wisdom reign,
And avoid the pitfalls of gambling's bane.

Final Flight

In the boundless sky, a pilot's domain,
A hero's journey, a test of the sane,
With courage and skill, he took to the air,
On wings of steel, without a despair.

Aboard the plane, passengers unaware,
Of the danger ahead, in the thin, crisp air,
A mechanical fault, a sudden descent,
Threatened to shatter their lives, their intent.

With calm and composure, the pilot's command,
He gripped the controls, his fate in his hand,
He fought against gravity's relentless pull,
To save every soul on that flight in full.

The engines screamed, the cockpit aglow,
As he battled the forces, both high and low,
With sweat on his brow, and a heart full of fire,
He steered through the storm, a celestial mire.

Through turbulence wild, he guided the way,
With nerves of steel, he held chaos at bay,
A dance in the sky, a dangerous fight,
To protect those on board, in the perilous night.

In a thunderous roar, they broke through the
cloud,
A moment of triumph, both thrilling and proud,
But as heroes go, in their selfless quest,
He paid the price, as fate's final test.

With the plane safe and all lives preserved,
The pilot's sacrifice, his legacy observed,
For he knew in his heart, as he faced the
unknown,
In saving them all, he had truly flown.

As the plane landed gently, on solid ground,
A hero's silence, an absence profound,
He had given his all, with courage and grace,
In the endless expanse of the sky's embrace.

A tale of valor, of a pilot's last flight,
A beacon of hope in the darkest of night,
In the annals of heroism, his name shall reside,
A guardian of skies, forever in flight.

Easy Come, Easy Go

In the shadows of the city's heart,
Lived a man, with life torn apart,
Homeless, he wandered, his dreams long gone,
A soul forgotten, by the world withdrawn.

But fate, a fickle and curious friend,
Decided to twist and to bend,
The path of this man, his fortune to change,
In a lottery ticket, a chance to exchange.

The numbers aligned, his ticket a prize,
A fortune that glittered before his eyes,
He stepped from the streets to the lap of luxury,
A world of excess, a newfound decree.

With mansions and cars, and parties galore,
He spent his wealth, and then he spent more,
But in the glitter and shine of a life anew,
He forgot the lessons that life once knew.

As quickly as fortune had found its way,
It vanished like smoke in the light of day,
The riches were gone, his treasures all spent,
And he found himself back where his journey
had begun.

Homeless once more, he faced the cold,
A sobering truth, a story retold,
In his quest for more, he'd lost his way,
The lottery's fortune had led him astray.

A cautionary tale, of the twists of fate,
Of how one's life can quickly abate,
In the cycle of life, we must all be aware,
That wealth can vanish, and leave us in despair.

For the true riches lie not in gold,
But in the love and warmth we hold,
In the hearts of others, in compassion's embrace,
In the simple joys of life's humble grace.

Charm City

In Baltimore's embrace, my childhood unfurled,
A city of stories, where memories swirl,
From Inner Harbor's charm to Chesapeake's
shores,
In the heart of Maryland, my spirit soars.

By the water's edge, where history resides,
The Inner Harbor gleams, with endless tides,
Tall ships and museums, a bustling core,
A place where the past and present are explored.

I strolled along the promenade's delight,
With cityscape views in the soft twilight,
The smell of seafood and the sounds of the bay,
In Baltimore's heart, where I longed to stay.

At Orioles games, with cheers and delight,
I wore the orange with pride, under stadium
lights,
From Camden Yards' roar to a home run's cry,
In baseball's embrace, I felt sky high.

And Ravens games, with a sea of purple and
black,
The thunderous roar, the fans in full attack,

In M&T Bank Stadium's electric embrace,
I learned the meaning of Baltimore's grace.

But crabs, oh crabs, the city's true delight,
Steamed in Old Bay seasoning, a taste so right,
With mallets and newspapers spread on the
floor,
We feasted on crabs, forever wanting more.

So, here's to my city, my Baltimore dear,
Where memories linger, crystal and clear,
In the charm of the harbor, the crabs, and the
games,
I grew up in Baltimore, the place The Wire gave
fame.

Happiness Is...

Dancing in the moonlight's glow,
Eager laughter, hearts flow,
Eclipsing worries, let them go,
Zest for life, a vibrant show.

Nurturing dreams, we find our way,
Unleashing joy throughout the day,
Taking chances, come what may,
Savoring moments, we shall play.

Read The Room

There once was a boy from the town,
Who thought he'd found love all around,
A girl kept on staring,
His heart started daring,
Till he saw his zipper was down!

Forbidden Love

In shadows' veil, forbidden love's embrace,
A man entangled in a web of grace,
He hides his heart, a secret burdened, deep,
For she, another's, her commitment to keep.

Her beauty, like a moonbeam's gentle glow,
He longs for her, but cannot let it show,
In stolen glances, their worlds collide,
Yet in his heart, his love he cannot hide.

He dreams of moments that can never be,
A life entwined, a love kept secretly,
But honor's call, a conscience takes its stand,
For love unbidden, may scar both heart and
hand.

In silence, he must bear this heavy weight,
A love that's destined to remain a silent fate,
For in his heart, he knows the painful truth,
That love, unfulfilled, can age a soul like youth.

A Kid With A Dream

A kid with a dream,
To lead the country supreme,
He worked hard every day,
To make his dream come true one day.

He studied and learned,
And his passion burned,
For the country he loved,
And the people thereof.

Years went by,
And he reached for the sky,
He became the President,
And led with great intent.

He made the country great,
And it was his fate,
To be remembered forevermore,
As a leader who opened many doors.

But then he woke up one day,
And realized it was all just play,
A dream that he had dreamed,
But it was not as it seemed.

He smiled and laughed,
At the dream that had passed,
But he knew in his heart,
That he had played a great part.

Even though it was just a dream,
It was more than it seemed,
It was a vision of what could be,
If we all worked together, you see.

In A World...

In a world where shadows loomed and night was
long,
A darkness fell, and hope seemed all but gone,
Amidst the chaos, in a city's gloom,
A lone survivor, a flicker in the doom.

The streets once filled with life, now barren,
stark,
Echoed with whispers of the undead's dark,
Their moans resounded like thunder's might,
A ceaseless craving, relentless, and tight.

At dawn's first light, the battle would begin,
To face the hordes, to conquer fear within,
With makeshift weapons, courage on display,
A survivor rose to greet the fateful day.

Through shattered buildings, they'd make their
stand,
United souls in this desolate land,
Each step they took, each breath they drew,
In the name of survival, they'd carry through.

With every heartbeat, with every sigh,

They fought for freedom 'neath the blood-red
sky,
But in their midst, a traitor hid,
A survivor turned, their hopes forbid.

Betrayal's venom, a twist untold,
In the darkest hours, when trust grew cold,
Yet in their unity, they found their way,
To forge a path to a brighter day.

Through battles fierce, and endless strife,
They clung to hope, to the spark of life,
As night receded, and dawn did break,
They knew they'd triumph, for humanity's sake.

And when the final battle had been won,
When the dawn's first light revealed the sun,
Survivors they stood, with scars imprinted deep,
In a reborn world, where their strength took a
leap.

In the face of darkness, they'd found the light,
In the midst of horror, they'd won the fight,
A tale of survival, where courage unfurled,
In the midst of the zombie apocalypse, they'd
conquered the world.

The Food Truck

Beneath the moon's pale, shivering gleam,
A food truck lurks, a spectral dream,
Its wheels screech softly on the night,
Where souls in need await their bite.

In the city's shadows, where despair resides,
A vendor's heart, with compassion abides,
With spoon and pot, he stirs and steams,
Nourishing hopes in his nightly schemes.

The homeless gather in the frigid air,
Their faces are lined with burdens they bear,
Yet in this darkness, a beacon shines bright,
A food truck offering solace in the night.

His soups and stews, a warming grace,
In the midst of hunger, they find their place,
A refuge from the cold, a respite from strife,
In the food truck's embrace, they renew their
life.

With ladle in hand, the vendor bestows,
Not just a meal, but the compassion that flows,
In the depths of the night, where shadows loom,
He serves humanity, dispelling the gloom.

Though his life's not grand, his mission is clear,
To feed the hungry, to calm their fear,
In the spirit of Poe, a tale unfolds,
Of a food truck's warmth in the winter's cold.

Amidst the urban core, where struggles persist,
The food truck's compassion, a heart's gentle
twist,
A tale of humanity, where darkness may roam,
But in the food truck's light, they find a home.

A Burning Desire

In a world ablaze with dreams and schemes,
I carry a fire, where my spirit gleams,
A burning desire, a relentless creed,
To see everyone rise, to succeed.

In the heart of the struggle, I find my grace,
With an unwavering hope for every face,
For in unity's tapestry, we all intertwine,
And together, we can make the stars align.

I want to see you rise, break through the skies,
With dreams unfurled, and purpose in your eyes,
To shatter the chains that hold you tight,
And emerge as a beacon in the darkest night.

In the face of challenges, we'll find our might,
With resilience and courage, we'll take flight,
With each person's success, the world grows
bright,
A symphony of dreams, a shared delight.

So let's lift each other, no matter the cost,
In unity's embrace, we won't be lost,
With a burning desire, a flame that won't recede,
Together, we'll triumph, together, we'll succeed.

In this world of hope, where dreams are a seed,
I carry a fire, a relentless creed,
To see everyone rise, to achieve,
For in your success, I truly believe.

The Writer's Journey

In a room of solitude, he'd often dwell,
A frustrated writer, his story to tell,
For years, he'd wrestled with the empty page,
His novel's journey, is like an endless cage.

The words, they danced, then slipped away,
Fleeting ideas, like the light of day,
Each sentence began, then cast aside,
In the tangled web, his dreams would hide.

His characters whispered, with untold tales,
Their voices were silenced by self-doubt's gales,
The novel's world, is a maze, a misty maze,
Yet he yearned to see the final phrase.

But as time flowed on, the seasons spun,
The writer's battles, were never won,
Then, in a moment, his words took flight,
The novel was born, in the soft moonlight.

The pages filled with stories long suppressed,
In his magnum opus, he'd given his best,
With a sense of fulfillment, he drew his last
breath,
As he penned the end, welcoming death.

The manuscript lay, a legacy profound,
A novel complete, on solid ground,
But the writer, he'd left, before it began,
Its journey into the world, across the land.

In the realm of words, his spirit soars,
The frustrated writer, whose passion implores,
Though he's gone from life, his tale is near,
For the novel lives on, his voice we'll hear.

In the pages of his work, his soul is found,
A story profound, forever unbound,
A tribute to the writer's unyielding endeavor,
Whose words will echo, in our hearts, forever.

L.O.V.E.

Let your heart ignite, so free and light,
Open to the beauty of each day, so bright,
View the world with wonder, free from strife,
Embrace the moments, cherish love in life.

Unbroken

In the silent echoes of my soul's embrace,
I hold a love, both tender and base,
A bond that time nor words can ever sever,
The love I feel for you, my brothers, forever.

In childhood's laughter and youthful strife,
We forged a connection, the rhythm of life,
Through the storms and the sun's warm reign,
Our shared moments are etched like an enduring
chain.

Though words may falter, and silence may
persist,
In my heart's chamber, your love exists,
In your triumphs and moments of despair,
I'm there with you, to show I truly care.

With each passing day, our lives unfold,
Through stories untold, some solid some gold,
My dedication to you, my brothers in kind,
Is written in the echoes of my heart and mind.

So know, in the silence, in the depths of my soul,
In the whispers and in the unspoken role,
The love I hold for you, steadfast and true,
Is a testament to the bonds that forever ensue.

Dear Mama

In the crucible of life, she stood so strong,
A single mother, against the odds, so long,
She toiled and strived, with love as her guide,
For her children's dreams, she'd never let slide.

With determination etched in every line,
She toiled through darkness, her love so divine,
Through sleepless nights, with hope in her view,
She lit the path for dreams to come true.

She was a teacher, wise and kind,
Imparting knowledge to young hearts and minds,
Then, in the post office's steady flow,
She worked for years, but there was more to
sow.

She returned to teaching, her passion ablaze,
Guiding students through life's intricate maze,
Touching lives, as she'd always done,
With her wisdom, like the morning sun.

Her dedication, a beacon so bright,
In the classroom's embrace, she'd shine her light,
A mentor to many, a source of grace,
Leaving an indelible mark in life's embrace.

Her hands, weathered and strong, her heart pure
gold,
Forging pathways to futures untold,
With cakes she baked and tables she'd spread,
Feeding not just her own, but many families
ahead.

Her children's success, a testament bright,
To her love, her strength, her endless fight,
For every trial, for every tear,
She was their rock, their source of cheer.

So here's to the mother who gave her all,
To break down barriers, to answer the call,
You are loved more than words can ever show,
A debt of gratitude, more than you'll ever know.

In your selfless love, your enduring grace,
You've made our lives, a wondrous place,
For the sacrifices you've made, the love you've
shown,
A single mother's heart, we'll forever own.